Animal Classifications

# Invertebrates

Angela Royston

heinemann raintree

© 2015 Heinemann Raintree
an imprint of Capstone Global Library, LLC
Chicago, Illinois

To contact Capstone Global Library, please call
800-747-4992, or visit our web site www.capstonepub.com

All rights reserved. No part of this publication may be reproduced or transmitted in any form or by any means, electronic or mechanical, including photocopying, recording, taping, or any information storage and retrieval system, without permission in writing from the publisher.

Edited by Helen Cox Cannons, Clare Lewis, and
Abby Colich
Designed by Steve Mead
Picture research by Tracy Cummins
Production by Victoria Fitzgerald
Originated by Capstone Global Library Ltd

**Library of Congress Cataloging-in-Publication Data**
Royston, Angela, 1945- author.
Invertebrates / Angela Royston.
pages cm—(Animal classification)
Summary: "This fascinating series takes a very simple look at animal classifications, with each book focusing on a different group of animal. This book is about invertebrates: what they do, how they behave, and how these characteristics are different from other groups of animals. Beautifully illustrated with colorful photographs, the book shows many examples of different types of invertebrates in their natural environment."—Provided by publisher.
Includes bibliographical references and index.
ISBN 978-1-4846-0752-7 (hb)—ISBN 978-1-4846-0759-6 (pb)—ISBN 978-1-4846-0796-1 (ebook) 1. Invertebrates—Juvenile literature. 2. Animals—Classification—Juvenile literature. I. Title.

QL362.4.R69 2015
592—dc23 2014013459

**This book has been officially leveled by using the F&P Text Level Gradient™ Leveling System.**

**Acknowledgments**
We would like to thank the following for permission to reproduce photographs: iStock: AtWaG, 6; Science Source: D.P. Wilson/FLPA, 23; Shutterstock: Bennyartist, 10, Bonnie Taylor Barry, 13, Borisoff, 27, Denis Vesely, 12, 29 (top), EcoPrint, 11, 29 (bottom), Edwin van Wier, 4, Fotochip, 17, Igor Gorelchenkov, cover, ILeysen, 25, Klagyivik Viktor, 16, Litvintsev Ihor, 7, Marinerock, 14, Mauro Rodrigues, 19, 29 (middle), MaZiKab, 21, Melola, 15, Mirvav, 18, ninii, 5, Protasov AN, design element (facet eye), RazvanZinica, 20, Rich Carey, 8, val lawless, 24, Vlad61, 26, yevgeniy11, 22, 28; SuperStock: Dave Fleetham/Pacific Stock - Design Pics, 9.

We would like to thank Michael Bright for his invaluable help in the preparation of this book.

Every effort has been made to contact copyright holders of material reproduced in this book. Any omissions will be rectified in subsequent printings if notice is given to the publisher.

All the Internet addresses (URLs) given in this book were valid at the time of going to press. However, due to the dynamic nature of the Internet, some addresses may have changed, or sites may have changed or ceased to exist since publication. While the author and publisher regret any inconvenience this may cause readers, no responsibility for any such changes can be accepted by either the author or the publisher.

Printed in the United States 5877

# Contents

Meet the Invertebrates ..... 4
Animals with Shells ..... 6
Squids and Octopuses ..... 8
Crabs, Lobsters, and Shrimps ..... 10
Insects ..... 12
From Caterpillar to Butterfly ..... 14
Living Together ..... 16
Spiders and Scorpions ..... 18
Many Legs ..... 20
Worms ..... 22
Jellyfish ..... 24
Incredible Coral ..... 26
Quiz ..... 28
*Glossary* ..... 30
*Find Out More* ..... 31
*Index* ..... 32

Some words are shown in bold, **like this**. You can find out what they mean by looking in the glossary.

# Meet the Invertebrates

Scientists divide living things into groups. This is called **classification**. A starfish and a ladybug do not look much alike, but they belong to the same huge group of animals. This group is called the **invertebrates**. Invertebrates do not have a backbone inside their bodies.

A starfish lives at the bottom of the sea.

A ladybug is an insect with wings and six legs.

Invertebrates are **classified** into many smaller groups, such as insects. Each group is different from other groups in particular ways.

# Animals with Shells

Some **invertebrates** have soft bodies. They are called **mollusks.** Some mollusks build a strong shell around their bodies. The shell protects the animal's body and gives it its shape. Limpets, mussels, and oysters are all mollusks that live in water.

Mussels and limpets cling to rocks.

A snail has two eyes, one at the end of each eyestalk.

A snail is a mollusk too. A snail carries its shell on its back as it moves along. If it is scared, it pulls its head and its one large foot back into the shell.

# Squids and Octopuses

Squids and octopuses are **mollusks,** even though they do not have a shell! Some squids are very large. They have eight arms and two **tentacles.** Giant squids grow up to 59 feet (18 meters) long.

A squid uses its two tentacles to catch food.

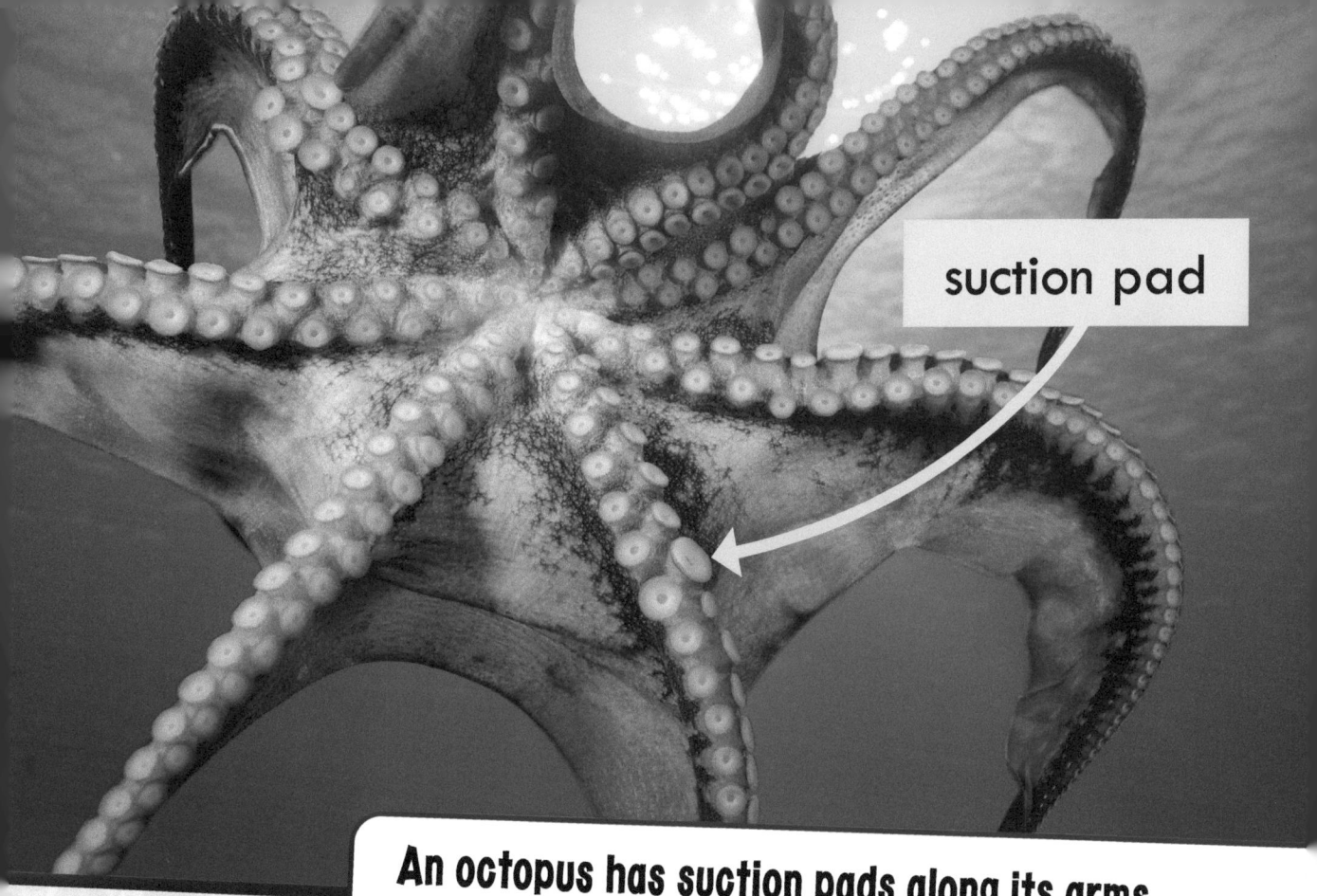


An octopus has suction pads along its arms. It uses them to grasp food and rocks.

Octopuses and squids can move fast by using their bodies like a **jet engine.** For example, an octopus pushes water backward out of its body so that it can shoot forward!

# Crabs, Lobsters, and Shrimps

Crabs, lobsters, and shrimps belong to a group of **invertebrates** called **crustaceans.** Their bodies are covered by a hard **skeleton,** like a suit of armor.

Almost every part of a shrimp's body is protected by its skeleton.

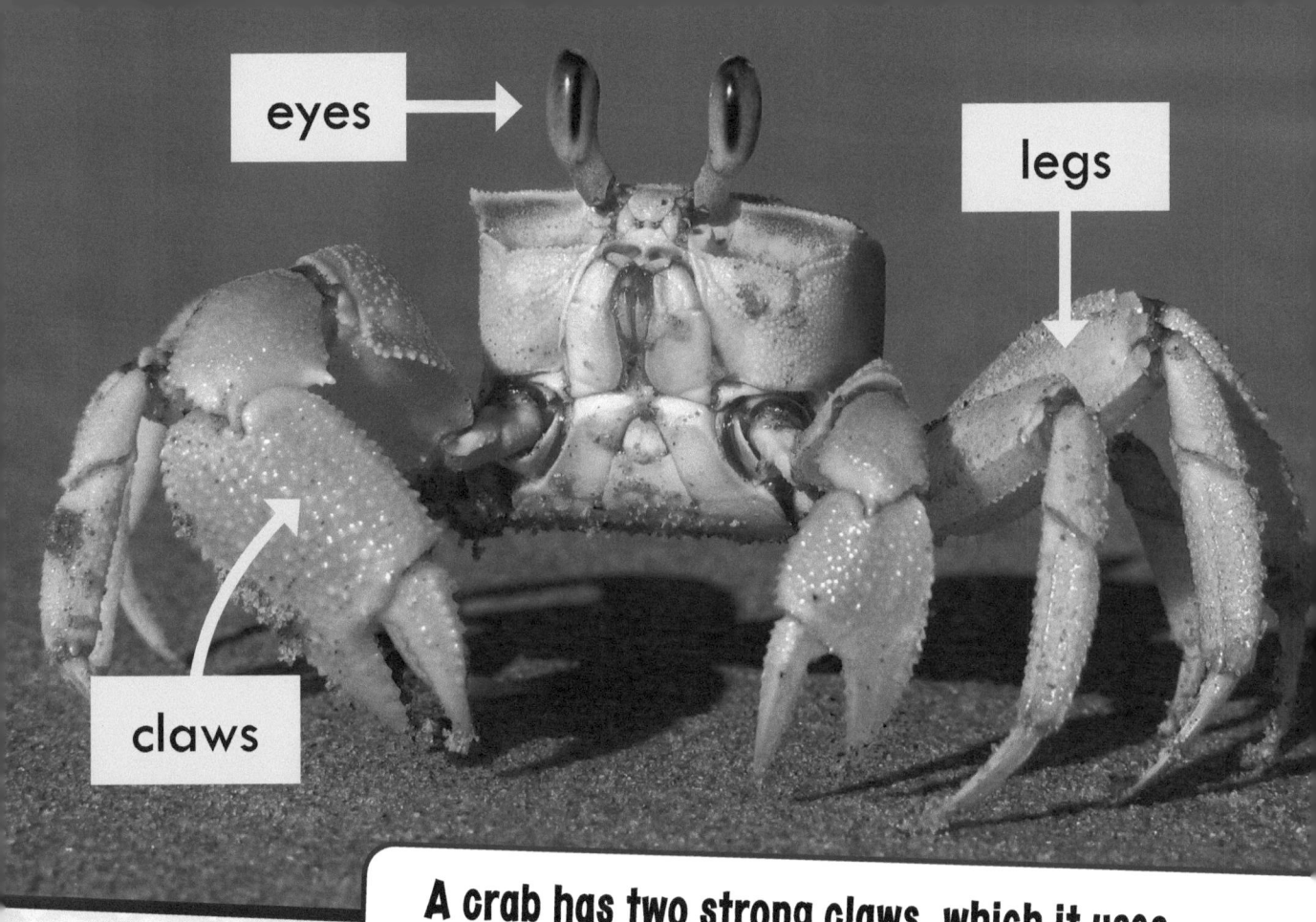


A crab has two strong claws, which it uses for fighting and for crushing food.

A crustacean's outer skeleton is made up of many parts, which fit together at the **joints.** Even a crustacean's long legs are protected by its skeleton. Some crabs walk sideways, because that is how their legs bend!

# Insects

The largest group of **invertebrates** is insects. They include dragonflies, beetles, and grasshoppers. Like **crustaceans**, insects have a hard outer **skeleton.**

**A grasshopper can fly, but it can also jump using its long back legs.**

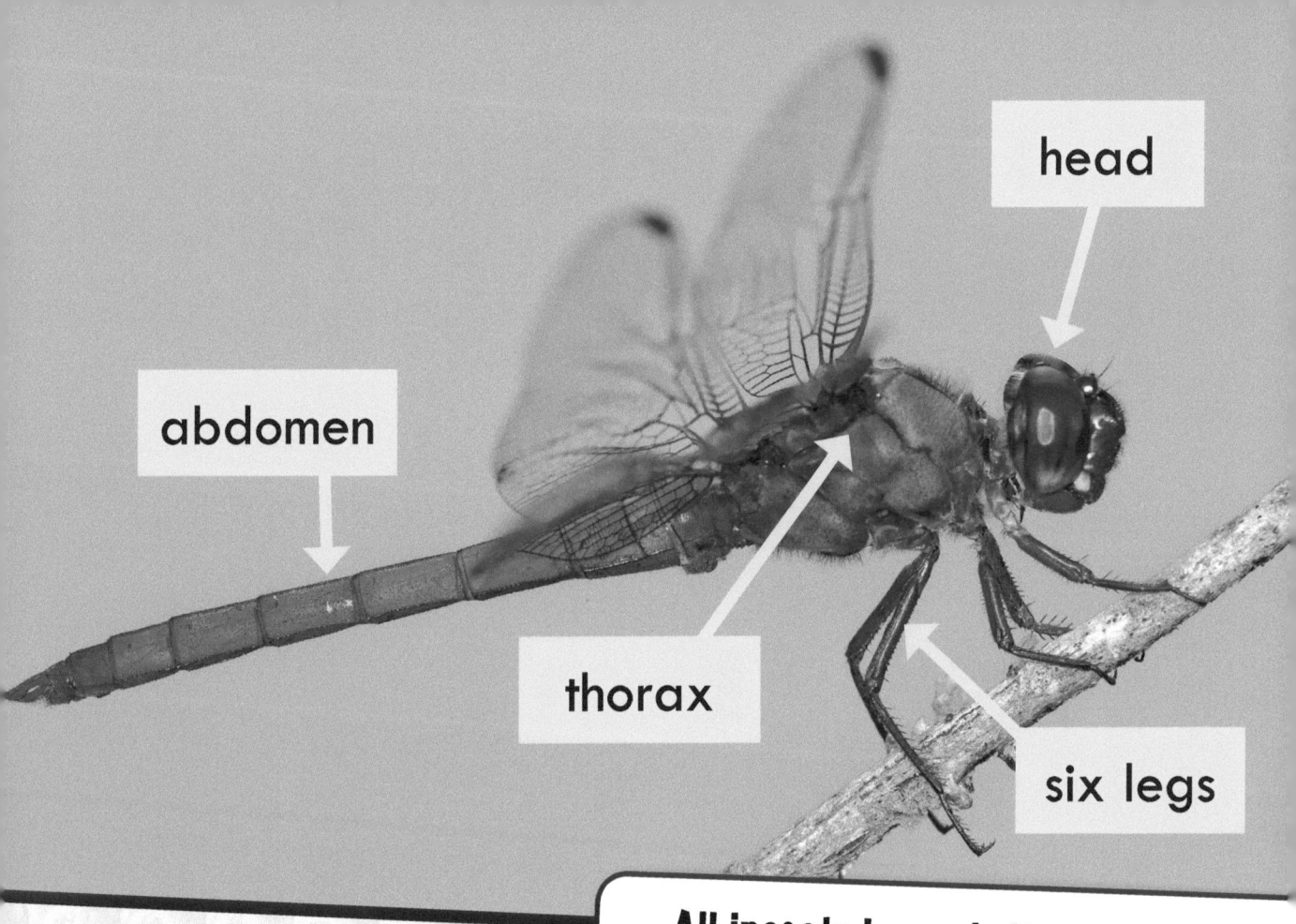


All insects have similar bodies.

All adult insects have six legs. Their bodies are divided into three parts: a head, thorax, and abdomen. Some insects have two pairs of wings, and some have one pair. Some insects have no wings at all.

# From Caterpillar to Butterfly

Many young insects look very different from adult insects. A caterpillar is a young butterfly. When the caterpillar is fully grown, it changes. The change is called **metamorphosis.**

A caterpillar eats and grows. Its favorite food is the leaf it **hatched** on.

As it changes, the caterpillar fixes itself to a leaf and sheds its skin. Under the skin is a kind of shell called a **pupa**. Inside the pupa, the caterpillar slowly becomes a butterfly.

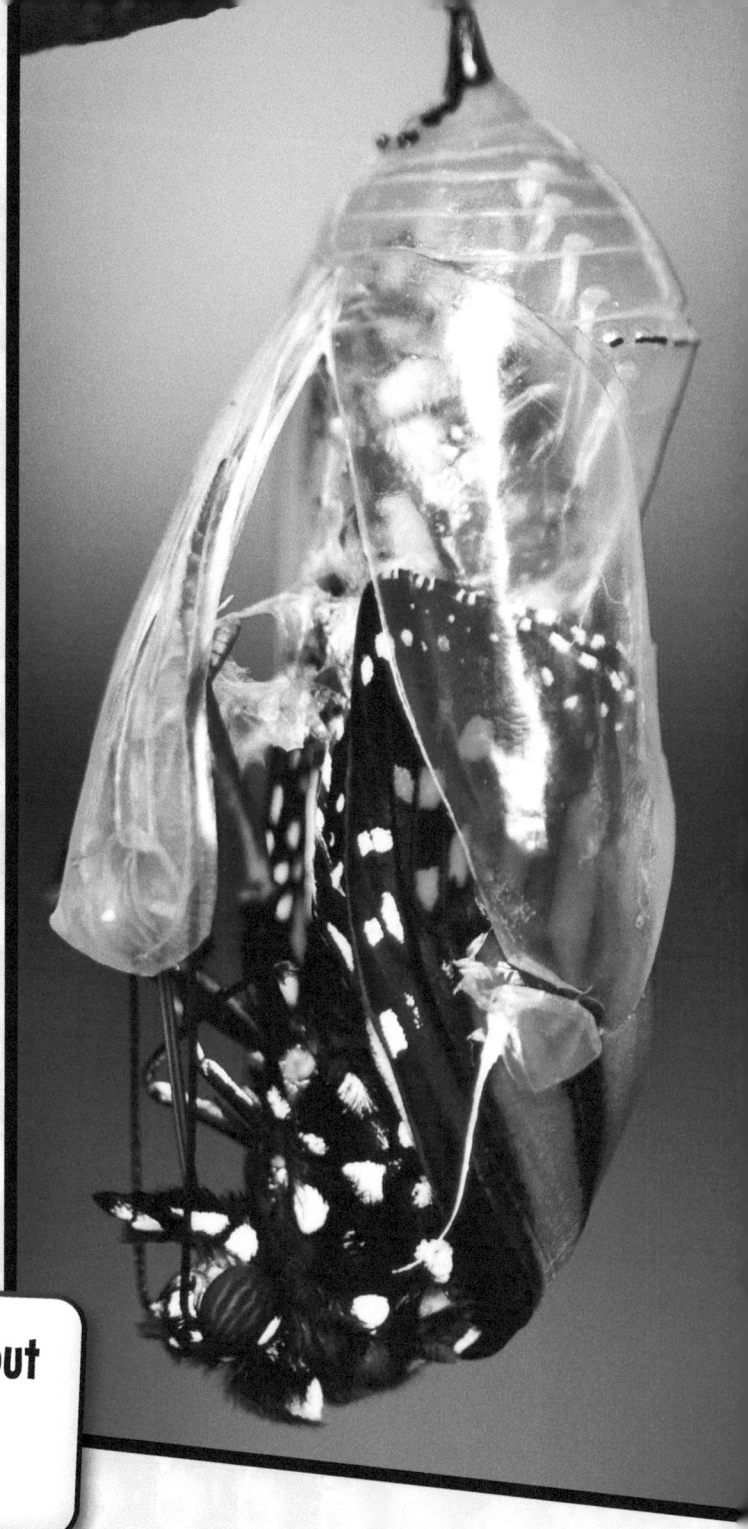

A butterfly breaks out of its pupa and gets ready to fly.

# Living Together

Many insects live alone, but some live together in large groups. They include ants and some bees and wasps. The queen is the main insect in a group. For example, a queen honeybee sets up a nest with many worker bees.

**Bees visit flowers to collect pollen and a sweet juice called nectar.**

Bees make honey inside the nest.

The worker bees collect **pollen** and **nectar** from flowers. They feed the queen bee with nectar and store the pollen to make honey. Only the queen lays eggs, which **hatch** into new bees.

# Spiders and Scorpions

It is easy to tell a spider from an insect. A spider has eight legs, a head, a body, and no wings. Most spiders feed on insects or other spiders.

Some spiders spin a web of silk thread to trap their prey.

A scorpion has a long tail, which it often curves over its back.

Scorpions have eight legs and belong to the same group as spiders. A scorpion has a **venomous** stinger at the end of its tail.

# Many Legs

Centipedes have up to 354 legs, although most have about 30 legs. Centipedes live in the soil. They are fierce hunters and feed at night on insects and spiders.

A centipede can run as fast backward as it does forward.

A millipede curls up tight when it is in danger.

Millipedes have up to 750 legs—even more than centipedes. Millipedes also come out at night and feed mainly on rotting plants. Most millipedes live in the soil or among dead leaves on the ground.

# Worms

Worms have no legs. Some worms live on the seashore. Others live in the soil. Earthworms feed on dead leaves and help to keep the soil healthy.

**Earthworms swallow dead plants and turn them into soil.**

Tube worms live around hot spots on the ocean bed.

Tube worms are some of the strangest animals. They live on the ocean bed and in the rotting bodies of dead whales. Giant tube worms can grow up to 6 and a half feet (almost 2 meters) long.

# Jellyfish

Jellyfish, sea anemones, and corals belong to the same group. They all have **tentacles** and a mouth in the middle of their soft, jelly-like body.

A sea anemone looks more like a plant than an animal.

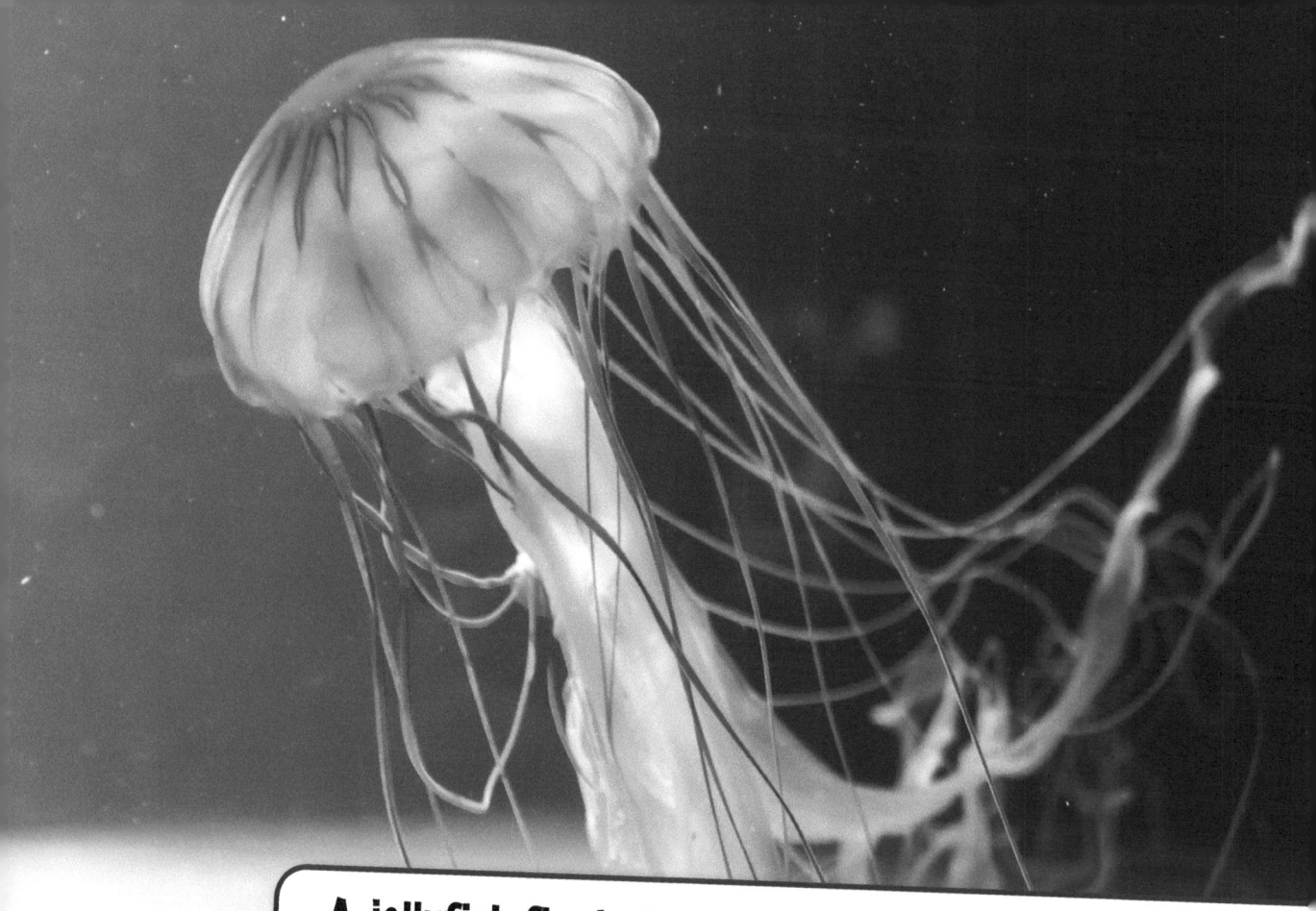

A jellyfish floats through the water. It uses its tentacles to defend itself and to catch **prey**.

Some jellyfish have very long tentacles, which can be 100 feet (30 meters) or longer. The tentacles contain **venomous** stingers. Some jellyfish are so venomous they can harm a person.

# Incredible Coral

A coral reef is amazing. It is made by millions of tiny animals called **coral polyps**. The **skeletons** of polyps grow on top of old, empty skeletons. Over millions of years, the reef slowly gets bigger.

Coral reefs can be very colorful.

The Great Barrier Reef stretches 1,400 miles (2,300 kilometers) along the coast of Australia.

Coral reefs provide a home for many **invertebrates.** In fact, more types of sea animals live around coral reefs than anywhere else in the ocean.

# Quiz

Look at the pictures below and read the clues. Can you remember the names of these **invertebrates**? Look back in the book if you need help.

**1.** I have no legs and live in the soil. What am I?

Answers
1. worm
2. grasshopper
3. scorpion
4. crab

**2.** I have six legs and can jump as well as fly. What am I?

**3.** I have eight legs and a stinger in my tail. What am I?

**4.** I have a hard outer **skeleton** and two big claws. What am I?

# Glossary

**classification** system that scientists use to divide living things into separate groups

**classified** put into a group according to special things shared by that group

**coral polyp** tiny animal whose skeleton helps to build a coral reef

**crustacean** member of a group of invertebrates whose bodies, including their legs and claws, are covered with a hard, chalky skeleton

**hatch** break out of an egg

**invertebrate** member of a very large group of animals that do not have bones inside their bodies. Invertebrates do not have a backbone.

**jet engine** powerful machine that moves an airplane or boat forward by pushing air out of the back of the engine

**joint** place where two bones or pieces of hard shell meet. Joints allow legs and other body parts to move.

**metamorphosis** complete change in body shape that insects go through when the young become adults

**mollusk** member of a group of invertebrates, most of whom have a single shell or a double shell that protects their body

**nectar** sweet juice found in flowers

**pollen** fine yellow dust made by flowers

**prey** animal that is hunted by another animal for food

**pupa** stage an insect goes through when it changes from a caterpillar to a butterfly or moth

**skeleton** hard frame inside or outside the body that gives an animal its shape

**tentacles** long arms that an invertebrate uses to feel, to move, or to hold things

**venomous** full of venom. Venom is poison that is injected by a stinger.

# Find Out More

## Books

Berger, Melvin and Gilda. *Butterflies and Caterpillars* (True or False). New York: Scholastic, 2008.

Schuetz, Kari. *Insects* (Blastoff!: Animal Classes). Minneapolis: Bellwether Media, 2013.

Veitch, Catherine. *Bug Babies* (Animal Babies). Chicago: Heinemann Library, 2013.

# Index


ants 16

backbones 4
bees 16–17
butterflies 14, 15

caterpillars 14–15
centipedes 20, 21
classification 4, 5
coral reefs 24, 26–27
crabs 10, 11
crustaceans 10–11

dragonflies 12, 13

earthworms 22
eggs 17

grasshoppers 12
Great Barrier Reef 27

insects 5, 12–17, 18, 20

jellyfish 24–25

ladybugs 4, 5
limpets 6

lobsters 10

metamorphosis 14–15
millipedes 21
mollusks 6–9
mussels 6

nests 16

octopuses 8–9
oysters 6

pollen 16, 17
polyps 26
prey 18, 25
pupa 15

scorpions 19
sea anemones 24
shells 6–7, 8, 15
shrimps 10
skeletons 10, 11, 12, 26
snails 7
spiders 18, 19, 20
squids 8–9
starfish 4

tentacles 8, 24, 25
tube worms 23

venom 19, 25

wasps 16
wings 13
worms 22–23